The HOUSE Th

Editorial Offices: Glenview, Illinois • Parsippany, New Jersey • New York, New York

Sales Offices: Needham, Massachusetts • Duluth, Georgia • Glenview, Illinois • Coppell, Texas
Sacramento, California • Mesa, Arizona

By Anthony Lorenz 🔨 Illustrated by John Sandford

1

ISBN: 0-328-19174-4

7 8 9 10 V008 13

This is the architect who drew the plans for the house that Tony lives in.

These are the drivers
who delivered the
supplies to build the
house that Tony lives in.

5

These are the
construction workers
who built the house that
Tony lives in.

These are the electricians who installed the wires in the house that Tony lives in.

These are the plumbers
who connected the pipes
that bring the water to
the house that Tony lives in.

These are the painters
who painted the walls,
in the bedroom of the
house that Tony lives in.

13

These are the landscapers who planted the garden around the house that Tony lives in.

These are the movers who brought the furniture into the house that Tony lives in.

These are the neighbors who live next door to the house that Tony lives in.

This is Tony's family
who lives in the house
that Tony lives in.

This is...
the architect who drew the plans,
the drivers who delivered the supplies,
the construction workers who built the house,
the electricians who installed the wires,
the plumbers who connected the pipes,

the painters who painted the walls,
the landscapers who planted the garden,
the movers who brought the furniture,
the neighbors who live next door,
the family who loves Tony and the house that
    he lives in!